T0126186

RAINER MARIA RILKE

SONNETS TO ORPHEUS

Translation copyright © 2019 by Christiane Marks

First edition, 2019
All rights reserved

Library of Congress Cataloging-in-Publication Data: Available.
ISBN-13: 978-1-948830-06-5 / ISBN-10: 1-948830-06-X

*This project is supported in part by the New York State Council on the Arts
with the support of Governor Andrew M. Cuomo and the New York State Legislature.*

Printed on acid-free paper in the United States of America.

Text set in Garamond, a group of old-style serif typefaces
named after the punch-cutter Claude Garamont.

Cover Design by Anne Jordan and Mitch Goldstein
Interior Design by Anthony Blake

Open Letter is the University of Rochester's nonprofit, literary translation press:
Dewey Hall 1-219, Box 278968, Rochester, NY 14627

www.openletterbooks.org

RAINER MARIA RILKE

RILKE SONNETS TO ORPHEUS

SONNETS TO ORPHEUS

OPEN LETTER
LITERARY TRANSLATIONS FROM THE UNIVERSITY OF ROCHESTER

Dedicated to my large, wonderful, supportive family and circle of friends, but especially to the memory of my grandfather, Hermann Starke, who gave me my first Rilke volumes so many years ago, and to the memory of my father, Hans Buchinger, who read poetry aloud beautifully in several languages. And dedicated above all to my son, Noah Heringman, who first suggested that I translate these sonnets, and encouraged me every step of the way. *Dies ist unser Buch!*

FOREWORD

"All of my poems are about time," the Nobel Laureate Joseph Brodsky once noted, "about what time does to man." Inspired by the immortal god of song, Orpheus, as well as the all-too-mortal young ballerina, Wera Ouckama Knoop, Rainer Maria Rilke's *Sonnets to Orpheus* are also preoccupied with time—what expires in it as well as what endures beyond it:

> We are the driving ones.
> Yet, the way time goes by—
> see that as trivial,
> next to what stays.
>
> All that is rushing by,
> will be long over soon;
> only what then remains
> consecrates us. (1:22, ll. 1-8)

Christiane Marks's pellucid translations themselves are also about time—about how poems are absorbed and felt and understood over time. Encountering them, I was reminded of George Steiner's important apperception that literary translation is, among other things, the most sophisticated act of reading possible. These translations are the product of a life's attention to Rilke's masterwork. They embody and enact one of reading's greatest pleasures—that of returning to a text over time. Reading itself is also always an experience that occurs in time.

Poetic meter, of course, is also a kind of measuring of time, and one of the distinctions of Marks's translations is her palpable although light-handed attention to meter, aiming in particular to convey the predominantly dactylic verse of this sonnet sequence. Marks succeeds not only in capturing Rilke's music—often sacrificed in translation—but also in rendering his singular and indelible imagery, imagery obsessed with meditating about time, song, and listening, imagery that is always aiming to perceive things that are overlooked or hard to see:

> Mirrors: There's never been true description
> of what, in your innermost nature, you are.
> You, who seem made of the holes of sieves
> filled with the in-between spaces of time. (2:3, ll. 1-4)

Having spent considerable time now with these translations myself, I feel about them the way Rilke describes the rose: "to us you are the filled, the numberless blossom, / the object that's inexhaustible" (2:6, ll. 3-4). In a synesthetic moment of inspiration, Rilke likens its scent to sound. "For centuries now, your fragrance has called / over to us the sweetest of names," he writes (ll. 9-10). Christiane Marks's translations likewise call out and convey Rilke's poetry to a new generation, and "It suddenly fills the air like fame" (l.11).

—Jennifer Grotz

TRANSLATOR'S INTRODUCTION

Rainer Maria Rilke's fifty-five *Sonnets to Orpheus*, written down over a few days in an astonishing burst of inspiration, came to him in spoken form, as "an interior dictation, completely spontaneous."[1] And what student of modern poetry does not recall that the beginning of the first Duino Elegy was uttered by a voice calling out of the storm as the poet walked the ramparts of Duino Castle: "Who, if I cried out, would hear me from out of the ranks / of the angels?" (*Wer, wenn ich schriee, hörte mich denn aus der Engel / Ordnungen?*). The mysterious words even suggest the dactylic meter used in most of the elegies. The bulk of the Sixth and Ninth Elegies was imparted to Rilke by an inner voice as he walked home from the post office one day. Both the *Duino Elegies* and the *Sonnets to Orpheus*, composed simultaneously and considered by Rilke to be "of one birth," and "filled with the same essence," had their beginning in a very few weeks in February of 1922, in spoken form—as sound.[2]

When the Elegies were completed, Rilke made a point of not sending them to his dear friend and benefactor, Princess

Marie of Thurn and Taxis Hohenlohe, to whom they are dedicated, because he wanted her to *hear* them first, from his lips. Later, he wrote her that he did not recognize the full depth of his own sonnets until he had *read* them to her—again, experienced as sound.[3] He often walked up and down, away from his stand-up desk and back, in composing his poetry, which would have encouraged rhythmic composition.[4]

Since the sound and rhythm of his poetry were of such importance to Rilke, one of my first steps in translating them was to learn them by heart, so I would have them constantly accessible orally, even while ruminating on them away from my desk. Over the years, I spoke them to myself and occasionally to others in many different settings, open always to the mysterious message of sound and rhythm behind the "meaning," grateful to have been familiar with those particular sounds and rhythms since childhood, since I share Rilke's mother tongue. I tried to render the original not only accurately, but also in words chosen for sound, and metrically, since it is the meter which moves the poems along so beautifully. I did not have to render over-regular or mechanical-sounding meter, because Rilke uses it quite flexibly, often breaking the metric pattern to draw attention to special words and passages. However, he never wrote in free verse.

Many of these sonnets address the reader directly, personally—as did that spontaneous, inner dictation addressed to the poet. Quite a few of them begin with a familiar *du, dir* or *ihr* ("you," "to you," "you" plural) or commands: *horch, siehe, wolle* ("listen," "look," "wish for"). This immediacy accounts for much of the poems' appeal, as do the occasional colloquialisms like *und ob!, dass ihrs begrifft!, wie aber, sag' mir, soll,* and *wer weiss?* ("and how!"; "if only you could understand!"; "but how, tell me, can,"; and "who knows?") (I:3, I:5, I:16, II:20).

Occasional particularly important words and phrases are italicized, receiving the emphasis they might in conversation, which adds to the spoken, spontaneous feel. Italicized words and phrases occur in no fewer than 18 of the sonnets. Important examples include I:8: Jubel <u>weiss</u> ("Jubilation <u>knows</u>"); I:12: Die Erde <u>schenkt</u> ("they are earth's <u>gift</u>"); I:14: *Sind <u>sie</u> die Herrn* ("Are <u>they</u> the masters"); II:2: *den <u>wirklichen</u> Strich* ("the <u>true</u> line"); and II:2: *Zwar <u>war</u> es nicht* ("True, it did <u>not</u> exist.") In some cases, English syntax or meter has required a slight shift of the emphasis. Sonnet II:5, a particularly intense one, contains three italicized words: <u>so</u> *von Fülle übermannter* ("<u>so</u> completely"); <u>wieviel</u> *Welten* ("<u>countless</u> worlds"); and *aber <u>wann</u>* ("ah, but <u>when</u>"). This poem was inspired by a little anemone the poet had actually seen in a garden in Rome in 1914, and strongly identified with, as J. B. Leishman relates in his valuable notes on the Sonnets.[5] In Sonnet II:11 Rilke italicizes the whole line that sums up what he is saying about the human need to kill: *Töten ist eine Gestalt unseres wandernden Trauerns* ("Killing is just one form of our nomadic mourning"). It is simply a part of our often troubled, sometimes tragic, process of becoming. The reader/listener immediately feels involved; the poems, though cast in the traditional sonnet form, seem quite contemporary.

Preserving this fresh, spoken, quality became another important goal for me, particularly since it helps to reflect the poems' completely unanticipated, surprise arrival. Incidentally, Rilke had always depended on inspiration; he could not "force" creation. "The utmost" that he could do, he explained to a friend, was to prepare, and then wait.[6] This preparation included absolute solitude and inner openness, with perhaps some translation work and letter writing on the side.

In some of these sonnets there is a strange, one-time shift from the second to the third person, and these particular sonnets all begin in a similar way. For example, three begin with the direct-address form before making this shift: *Du aber, Herr* (I:20); *Du aber, Göttlicher* (II:7); *Tänzerin, o du Verlegung* (II:18). (The parallel is less obvious in translation: "What can I consecrate"; "But you, divine one"; "Dancer, how you have transmuted.") In each case, third-person pronoun phrases—"his evening," "when he was attacked," and "above her"—subsequently appear. Then, Rilke returns to the second person. Translators have generally circumvented or "corrected" these shifts by substituting the expectable second-person form. Yet these irregularities are surely not oversights, and so I have tried to preserve them. Rilke is showing the reader that in the world of these sonnets, it is possible to talk *to* someone and *about* someone to others at the same time, making the point that he has a large and diverse audience in mind, and an expanded definition of speech. Though more readily dismissed as mistakes, these switches from the second to the third person are no more accidental than coinages like *singender* and *preisender* (literally "more singingly" and "praisingly") which I render as "with stronger song" and "with more powerful praise" (II:13). The literally translated words seemed too odd for the poem, and the sound was not pleasing, so I have used alliteration to approximate the original emphasis. *Ins thorig offene Herz*, a phrase in which the noun "gate" (*das Thor*) has been boldly turned into an adjective, I render as "the gate-open heart" (II:9). Such idiosyncratic uses of German, of which there are quite a few in the sonnets, present a special challenge to the translator: while they should not be entirely smoothed over, their oddness must sometimes be tempered so it does not overwhelm the whole poem.

As already mentioned, Rilke uses meter flexibly. Here he begins an otherwise dactylic poem with three stresses together in a command: *In Schon, horch, hörst du die ersten Harken* (II:25) ("Come! Listen! Already you're hearing the first of the rakes"). Sonnet II:11 uses both metrical variation and enjambment for emphasis: *Leise liess man dich ein, als wärst du ein Zeichen / Frieden zu feiern. Doch dann: rang dich am Rande der Knecht.* ("Gently they lowered you; you seemed a signal to

celebrate / peace. But then the hired man shook your edge.")
Rilke emphasizes *Frieden* (peace) by beginning a new line with
the word. *Doch dann* ("but then"), two jolting stresses together
in mid-line, introduce the pivotal statement that not peace, but
killing is intended.

The sonnets in this much-loved cycle stand out in sonnet
history for their formal variety, and might for this reason seem
unaccustomed to those expecting only iambic pentameter, the
standard English sonnet meter since before Shakespeare. Only
eight of the *Sonnets to Orpheus* use this meter, including, how-
ever, four of the first five, which introduce the cycle—I:1,2,3,
and 5—as well as I:14, II:4, II:14, and II:27. Though all the
sonnets consist of two quatrains and two tercets, Sonnets I:9,
17, 18, 22, and 23 have only two or three beats per line, follow-
ing the short-line sonnet form popular in France at the time,
which Rilke admired in the work of Gide, Valery, and others. A
few sonnets like II:10, 17, and 19, on the other hand, are writ-
ten in hexameter lines; occasionally there will even be a seven
or eight-beat line, usually used to build up tension or suspense.
Irregular dactylic meter predominates throughout. Trochaic
meter is less used, though still eight times—in Sonnets I:8, 11,
12, and 13, and in II:5, 16, 23, 29. The important final sonnet
uses this somewhat solemn meter. Two particularly exuberant
sonnets—I:20 and II:12, about a runaway horse and the power
of transformation—are lifted and carried by dactylic meter.

In II:11 and 19, Rilke shortens the final lines of two poems in hexameter by half, to bring them to a close gradually and add additional weight to the final words. These are just a few examples of the ways in which Rilke puts meter to work for him, given because, at a time when some readers have become less conscious of the possibilities of meter, or consider it dated, I have chosen to duplicate the original meter. The meter is integral to these thoroughly modern poems—a part of their "message"—and Rilke's natural way of composing.

My enthusiasm for the vision behind these sonnets helped me decisively in trying to render the life and beauty of the originals. Rilke's visions simply ring true to me. As he explained to his Polish translator, he wrote both the Sonnets and the Elegies out of a growing belief in a great, unified wider world or "circulation," a belief that had finally enabled him to re-affirm his life, envision a future, and begin composing anew after the devastating years of World War I. That breakthrough, which came along with the unexpected sonnets, was real and vivid to me. Rilke became convinced that

> We who are alive here today are not satisfied with the temporal world—not for one moment. We are continually merging with those who came before us and those who appear to be coming after us. . . . In that greatest, that "open" world, all exist—we cannot say "at the same

time," since it's just because there is no time that they may all be there together. . . . The temporal, the transitory, plunges everywhere into deep being.[7]

In the Second Duino Elegy, Rilke writes that in this timeless realm angels do not even distinguish between the living and the dead: "Angels (they say) often don't know if they're walking / with the living or dead. The eternal current / sweeps through both realms all ages / ever along with it, its song drowning out theirs." (*Engel (sagt man) wüssten oft nicht, ob sie unter / Lebenden gehn oder Toten. Die ewige Strömung / reisst durch beide Bereiche alle Alter / immer mit sich und übertönt sie in beiden.*) Rilke's response to the slaughter of the war was to begin to see death not as the opposite of life, or complete annihilation, but simply as "the side of life that's turned away from and un-illuminated by us."[8] We must try our hardest to illuminate it with our consciousness, he stressed, which will remove our fear of it and help us to see that we are constantly nourished by both life and death together. Even in his twenties, Rilke had already held a positive view of death: "For we are only rind and leaf. / The great death which each life contains—/ that death's the fruit, around which all else turns." (*Denn wir sind nur die Schale und das Blatt. / Der grosse Tod, den jeder in sich hat, / das ist die Frucht, um die sich alles dreht.*)[9]

Death, to Rilke, was truly just life in another, non-physical state. One of two convictions, then, that decisively influenced the creation of the Sonnets was that the barriers between the states of life and death should be removed. The other was that love must find new roles within this wider whole that no longer simply excludes death as "the other."[10] Love enters the Sonnets in the form of praise and joyful affirmation of everything they touch—gardens, dancers, flowers, flavors, unicorns, the sense of hearing—whatever it might be. Even Rilke's machine sonnets (I:18, 22, 24 and II:10) are beautiful and show mechanization—of which he was deeply suspicious—as an opportunity for growth: we must remain the masters of the machines we have created. The most striking example of the power of love is found in Sonnet II:4, in which the mythical unicorn is "loved" into reality by those who believe in it.

The world of the sonnets is that of Orpheus himself, to whom they are addressed, in which song, beauty, and harmony reign eternally; his music charms even wild beasts. These are examples of a few of the many references to this ideal, ageless world in the Sonnets:

- Orpheus, the supreme poet and singer, dies many times, yet remains alive and present among us (I:5).

- We must keep in mind a lasting, crucial image—arguably the memory of this ideal world—even though it may be blurred from day to day (I:16).

- We are nourished by the lives of those who came before us (I:14).

- What is of lasting value comes from the elements of

our world not subject to time (I:22)

- Orpheus, the ultimate poet/singer, survives physical destruction (I:26).

- Love is the power that creates lasting reality (II:4).

- Flavor, fragrance, and music transcend everyday reality (I:15, II:6, II:10).

- Blissful, unblemished gardens exist in an ideal realm, but for us to claim as our own (II:17, 21).

- There is a place where even mute creatures, like fishes, have their language (II:20).

For Rilke, this ideal world is not isolated up above, but found all throughout our beautiful earth, which the Ninth Duino Elegy urges us to love with all our might just as it is—and thus lift up and transform. It is a unified world Rilke is envisioning, without the dualities of life and death, heaven and earth, good and evil, body and spirit; in fact, he moved away from traditional Christianity largely because it tends to emphasize these dualities. He tells us that the angels of the Elegies are not Christian angels, but more like Islamic ones, and of course Orpheus is a pre-Christian figure.[11]

In order to unite dualities—to bring light and dark, earth and heaven, good and bad, body and soul together—the poet praises. He simply praises everything. That is his calling. A few months before the sonnets came to him, Rilke wrote a poetic dedication for a friend into the pages of his novel *Die Aufze-*

ichnungen des Malte Laurids Brigge (The Notebooks of Malte Laurids Brigge) which began, "Oh, tell me, poet, what you do. I praise" (*O sage, Dichter, was du tust. Ich rühme*). It was the inspired sonnets that restored to him the power to praise, and that made the completion of the Elegies possible. "Praise" (*das Rühmen, die Rühmung*) and "praiseworthy" (*rühmlich*) are key words in the Sonnets, especially in I:7, 8, 9. Here and there lament is mixed with the praise, as in the machine sonnets (I:18, 24 and II:10, 22, for example) and in at least one sonnet dealing with Wera's illness and death (I:15). Entirely untempered praise would not be believable. Sonnet I:8 clearly sets forth, however, that praise must always go along with lament: *Nur im Raum der Rühmung darf die Klage / gehn* ("Only where there's praise may lamentation / sound")—a mixture of emotions reminiscent of the Old Testament Psalms.

Orpheus could well inspire a poet trying to see life and death as equally real, interpenetrating states, since he entered the realm of the dead in search of Eurydice, and then returned to the world of the living, albeit without her. Wera Ouckama Knoop, the young dancer, dead at 19, to whom the cycle is dedicated, had just made a one-time transition. But due to her youth and love of life, and the creative, joyous nature of even her last months, Rilke, who had read Wera's mother's loving account of her illness and death, had a strong sense of her continued presence and felt an "obligation" to celebrate her short life. The qualities of transformation, flexibility, and flow—the ability to move among different states—are celebrated throughout the cycle, down to the last poem's last lines: "And when earthly things forget you, / to the still earth say, 'I'm flowing.' / To the rushing water say, 'I am'" (*und wenn dich das Irdische vergass / zu der stillen Erde sag: Ich rinne. / Zu dem raschen Wasser sprich: "ich bin."*).

Translating in this momentous context, this wider, more open realm, or "circulation," meant turning every German and especially every English word over twice. English was "the strangest, most remote language" to Rilke, and he was always most particular about how his poetry was presented, even in the original German. He wished it to be heard whenever possible and did not wish it to be set to music or illustrated. Rilke was a translator himself, and evidence from his letters shows that he was both a self-critical producer and a critical consumer of translations, because not only the sense, but also the sound of poetry mattered so much to him.[12] Yet Rilke's cordial relationship with two of his translators is clearly reflected in his letters—those to Swedish translator Inga Junghanns, and those to Witold von Hulewicz, his Polish translator, to whom he wrote the deepest and most helpful explanations of the Sonnets and Elegies that we have.[13]

In a Christmas letter to an old friend, Rilke had this to say about reading the *Sonnets to Orpheus*: "It is in the nature of these poems, condensed and abbreviated as they are (in the way they frequently state lyrical sums rather than listing the steps leading up to the solution), that they seem more amenable to being grasped intuitively by the like-minded reader than by what is called 'understanding.'"[14] The sonnets' enduring popularity, even in English—yes, that "strangest and most remote of languages"—shows that English-language readers are responsive to truths so deep that they can be felt directly—intuitively—bypassing explanation and analytical thought, and that poems that both embody and celebrate flexibility, flow, and transformation—the essence of life—may serve as welcome antidotes to over-structured, mechanized lives. The growing desire to "illuminate" death and re-integrate it into everyday life (from where funeral homes and hospitals have tended to remove it) is even evident among the general public in the growing home-death care and green-funeral movements. Finally, recognizing death as the fruit, the culmination of life, rather than just a medical accident, simply adds meaning to all of existence. Uplifting and celebrating the seemingly commonplace—things as diverse as a weed-filled open grave (I:10), a runaway horse (I:20), the act of breathing (II:1), and the sound of rakes in a field (II:25)—has always been the province of poetry.

The English poet J. B. Leishman first made these sonnets available to English-language readers in 1936. He preserved not only the meter but also the rhyme, which led to some overly archaic word choices and some twisted syntax and meaning, but his translation is still, overall, an astonishing feat. Leishman's lovingly detailed commentary on the sonnets is still unsurpassed because of his close study of Rilke's entire work, including his many letters, his wide-ranging knowledge of languages and world literature, and his strong engagement with the times, vision, and inner state out of which Rilke wrote these sonnets, only 14 years earlier. In spite of the multitude of other translations of these sonnets, their first translator still occupies a unique position as a near-contemporary of Rilke's as well as an outstanding poet and scholar.

These sonnets have sometimes been called "a balm for wounded souls" and, indeed, they were written by a poet who characterized himself as "taking every creaking of the floorboards to heart."[15] Rilke wrote a vast number of beautiful letters, which should be considered a part of his oeuvre; many do attest to his kindness and ability to comfort, but the sonnets reach far beyond that. They are "true song . . . carried by a different breath, / an aimless breath, blown in the god. A wind" (I:3). (*In Wahrheit singen, ist ein anderer Hauch / Ein Hauch um nichts. Ein Wehn im Gott. Ein Wind.*)

The *Sonnets to Orpheus* are still needed, and I am honored to have been able to open a new window on them, for old and new Rilke lovers alike.

—Christiane Marks

1. "Une dictée interieure toute spontanée." Letter to Jean Strohl, quoted in Donald Prater, *Ein klingendes Glas* (Hamburg: Rohwolt, 1989), 576.

2. Rainer Maria Rilke, *Briefe aus Muzot* (Leipzig: Insel, 1937), 372; cf. Prater, *Ein klingendes Glas*, 577.

3. Prater, *Ein klingendes Glas*, 577; Hermann Mörchen, *Rilkes Sonette an Orpheus* (Stuttgart: Kohlhammer, 1958), 8.

4. Prater, *Ein klingendes Glas*, 565.

5. J. B. Leishman, Rainer Maria Rilke, *Sonnets to Orpheus*, (London: Hogarth Press, 1947), 164.

6. Ulrich Fülleborn and Manfred Engel, eds., *Materialien zu Rainer Maria Rilke's Duineser Elegien* (Frankfurt: Suhrkamp, 1980), 199.

7. Rilke, *Briefe aus Muzot*, 373.

8. Rilke, *Briefe aus Muzot*, 371.

9. Rilke, *Sämtliche Werke* (Frankfurt: Insel, 1955), 1: 246.

10. Rilke, *Briefe aus Muzot*, 230.

11. Rilke, *Briefe aus Muzot*, 373.

12. Rilke, *Briefe aus Muzot*, 323, 312, 356.

13. Rilke, *Briefe aus Muzot*, 371.

14. Rilke, *Briefe aus Muzot*, 230.

15. Rilke, *Briefe aus Muzot*, 168.

1:1

Da stieg ein Baum. O reine Übersteigung!
O Orpheus singt! O hoher Baum im Ohr!
Und alles schwieg. Doch selbst in der Verschweigung
ging neuer Anfang, Wink und Wandlung vor.

Tiere aus Stille drangen aus dem klaren
gelösten Wald von Lager und Genist;
und da ergab sich, dass sie nicht aus List
und nicht aus Angst in sich so leise waren,

sondern aus Hören. Brüllen, Schrei, Geröhr
schien klein in ihrem Herzen. Und wo eben
kaum eine Hütte war, dies zu empfangen,

ein Unterschlupf aus dunkelstem Verlangen
mit einem Zugang, dessen Pfosten beben, –
da schufst du ihnen Tempel im Gehör.

1:1

There, see—a tree ascended. Pure transcendence!
Oh, Orpheus sings! Oh, tall tree in the ear!
And all was silent. Yet that silence yielded
beginnings, beckonings, and transformations.

Creatures of stillness issued from the clear,
wide-open forest filled with lairs and nests.
And it turned out that neither cunning
nor fear had caused this inner quiet,

but listening had. Bellow and shriek and roar
seemed small inside their hearts, and where just now
there'd scarcely been a hut to take this in—

a hidden refuge made of darkest longing,
the very doorposts of its entrance quaking—
you raised up temples for them in their ears.

1:2

Und fast ein Mädchen wars und ging hervor
aus diesem einigen Glück von Sang und Leier
und glänzte klar durch ihre Frühlingsschleier
und machte sich ein Bett in meinem Ohr.

Und schlief in mir. Und alles war ihr Schlaf.
Die Bäume, die ich je bewundert, diese
fühlbare Ferne, die gefühlte Wiese
und jedes Staunen, das mich selbst betraf.

Sie schlief die Welt. Singender Gott, wie hast
du sie vollendet, dass sie nicht begehrte,
erst wach zu sein? Sieh, sie erstand und schlief.

Wo ist ihr Tod? O, wirst du dies Motiv
erfinden noch, eh sich dein Lied verzehrte? –
Wo sinkt sie hin aus mir? ... Ein Mädchen fast ...

1:2

It was a girl, almost, who was engendered
by this one blended joy of song and lyre,
and shone out radiantly through veils of springtime
and made herself a bed inside my ear.

And slept in me. And she slept everything.
All trees that ever I admired, the distance
that I could feel, this meadow that I felt,
and all of my amazement at myself.

She slept the world. Say, singing god, how did you
create her so she did not wish to be
awake at first? For see, she rose and slept.

Where is her death? Oh, will you still complete
this theme before your song consumes itself?
She's sinking out of me . . . to where? A girl, almost . . .

1:3

Ein Gott vermags. Wie aber, sag mir, soll
ein Mann ihm folgen durch die schmale Leier?
Sein Sinn ist Zwiespalt. An der Kreuzung zweier
Herzwege steht kein Tempel für Apoll.

Gesang, wie du ihn lehrst, ist nicht Begehr,
nicht Werbung um ein endlich noch Erreichtes;
Gesang ist Dasein. Für den Gott ein Leichtes.
Wann aber *sind* wir? Und wann wendet er

an unser Sein die Erde und die Sterne?
Dies *ists* nicht, Jüngling, dass du liebst, wenn auch
die Stimme dann den Mund dir aufstösst, – lerne

vergessen, dass du aufsangst. Das verrinnt.
In Wahrheit singen, ist ein andrer Hauch.
Ein Hauch um nichts. Ein Wehn im Gott. Ein Wind.

1:3

A god can do it. But, how, tell me, can
a man pass through the slender lyre and follow?
His mind's in conflict, and where heart-ways cross
no one erects a temple for Apollo.

Song as it's taught by you is not desire,
does not court distant goals, barely achieved.
Singing is being. Easy for a god.
When will we truly *be*? And when does he

turn toward our being earth and stars?
Falling in love, young man, is *not* what matters, though
song then bursts from your lips. Learn to forget

such spasms of song. They have no permanence.
True song is carried by a different breath—
an aimless breath, blown in the god. A wind.

1:4

O ihr Zärtlichen, tretet zuweilen
in den Atem, der euch nicht meint,
lasst ihn an eueren Wangen sich teilen,
hinter euch zittert er, wieder vereint.

O ihr Seligen, o ihr Heilen,
die ihr der Anfang der Herzen scheint.
Bogen der Pfeile und Ziele von Pfeilen,
ewiger glänzt euer Lächeln verweint.

Fürchtet euch nicht zu leiden, die Schwere,
gebt sie zurück an der Erde Gewicht;
schwer sind die Berge, schwer sind die Meere.

Selbst die als Kinder ihr pflanztet, die Bäume,
wurden zu schwer längst; ihr trüget sie nicht.
Aber die Lüfte ... aber die Räume ...

1:4

Oh, you tender ones, sometimes place
your feet in the breath not intended for you.
Let it divide as it reaches your cheeks,
reuniting behind you, tremulously.

Oh, you blessed ones, oh, you whole ones,
you who seem the beginning of hearts.
bows for the arrows and targets of arrows,
you smile more eternally through your tears.

Don't be afraid to suffer. The weight,
add it back in with the weight of the earth.
Mountains are heavy, and heavy the seas.

You could not carry even the trees
that you planted as children. Too heavy they've grown.
Ah, but the ether . . . ah, but the spaces . . .

1:5

Errichtet keinen Denkstein. Lasst die Rose
nur jedes Jahr zu seinen Gunsten blühn.
Denn Orpheus ists. Seine Metamorphose
in dem und dem. Wir sollen uns nicht mühn

um andre Namen. Ein für alle Male
ists Orpheus, wenn es singt. Er kommt und geht.
Ists nicht schon viel, wenn er die Rosenschale
um ein paar Tage manchmal übersteht?

O wie er schwinden muss, dass ihrs begrifft!
Und wenn ihm selbst auch bangte, dass er schwände.
Indem sein Wort das Hiersein übertrifft,

ist er schon dort, wohin ihrs nicht begleitet.
Der Leier Gitter zwängt ihm nicht die Hände.
Und er gehorcht, indem er überschreitet.

1:5

Do not erect a marker. Let the rose
just bloom to honor him from year to year.
For it is he. His metamorphosis
in this thing and in this. We must not search

for other names. It's simply Orpheus
wherever there is song. He comes and goes.
And isn't it a lot when he outlasts
by several days, sometimes, the bowl of roses?

He has to vanish—can't you understand?
And even if he feared his vanishing.
Because his word transcends our here and now,

he is already where we cannot follow.
The lyre's fence does not obstruct his hands.
And this transgression is obedience.

1:6

Ist er ein Hiesiger? Nein, aus beiden
Reichen erwuchs seine weite Natur.
Kundiger böge die Zweige der Weiden,
wer die Wurzeln der Weiden erfuhr.

Geht ihr zu Bette, so lasst auf dem Tische
Brot nicht und Milch nicht; die Toten ziehts –.
Aber er, der Beschwörende, mische
unter der Milde des Augenlids

ihre Erscheinung in alles Geschaute;
und der Zauber von Erdrauch und Raute
sei ihm so wahr wie der klarste Bezug.

Nichts kann das gültige Bild ihm verschlimmern;
sei es aus Gräbern, sei es aus Zimmern,
rühme er Fingerring, Spange und Krug.

1:6

Is he from our world? No—it took two worlds
joining to form his expansive nature.
Those who have known the willow's deep roots,
they bend willow branches more expertly.

Going to bed, do not leave on the table
bread or milk. They draw back the dead.
But let the conjuror come and mingle,
mildly veiled by his half-closed eye,

their apparitions with all that we see;
may the magic of earthsmoke and rue be
as true to him as the clearest relation.

Nothing can spoil the true image for him.
Rings, pins, and pitchers, from graves and from dwellings—
all of them, equally, merit his praise.

1:7

Rühmen, das ists! Ein zum Rühmen Bestellter
ging er hervon wie das Erz aus des Steins
Schweigen. Sein Herz, o vergängliche Kelter
eines den Menschen unendlichen Weins.

Nie versagt ihm die Stimme am Staube
wenn ihn das göttliche Beispiel ergreift.
Alles wird Weinberg, alles wird Traube,
in seinem fühlenden Süden gereift.

Nicht in den Grüften der Könige Moder
straft ihn die Rühmung Lügen, oder
dass von den Göttern ein Schatten fällt.

Er ist einer der bleibenden Boten,
der noch weit in die Türen der Toten
Schalen mit rühmlichen Früchten hält.

1:7

Praise is what's called for! And summoned for praising
he issued forth like ore from the stone's
silence. His heart—oh, temporal wine press,
yielding for us inexhaustible wine.

His voice is never extinguished by dust
when he is seized by divine example.
All turns to vineyard, all turns to grape,
ripening in his sensuous south.

Royal decay in burial vaults,
shadows that sometimes the gods will cast—
never raise doubt toward his songs of praise.

He is one of the permanent messengers
holding far into the doors of the dead
vessels of praiseworthy fruit in his hands.

1:8

Nur im Raum der Rühmung darf die Klage
gehn, die Nymphe des geweinten Quells,
wachend über unserem Niederschlage,
dass er klar sei an demselben Fels,

der die Tore trägt und die Altäre. –
Sieh, um ihre stillen Schultern früht
das Gefühl, dass sie die jüngste wäre
unter den Geschwistern im Gemüt.

Jubel *weiss* und Sehnsucht ist geständig, –
nur die Klage lernt noch; mädchenhändig
zählt sie nächtelang das alte Schlimme.

Aber plötzlich, schräg und ungeübt,
hält sie doch ein Sternbild unserer Stimme
in den Himmel, den ihr Hauch nicht trübt.

1:8

Only where there's praise may lamentation
go, the naiad of the pool of tears,
keep the watch on our precipitation,
guard its clarity upon the very cliff

carrying the portals and the altars.
See, around her quiet shoulders dawns
the awareness that, of all the sisters
of the heart, she is the youngest one.

Joy already *knows*; longing admits.
Lamentation's learning still. Her girlish
hands count up old woes the whole night long.

Still, she raises suddenly, aslant,
awkwardly, our voice, as constellation
into heavens by her breath undimmed.

1:9

Nur wer die Leier schon hob
auch unter Schatten,
darf das unendliche Lob
ahnend erstatten.

Nur wer mit Toten vom Mohn
ass, von dem ihren,
wird nicht den leisesten Ton
wieder verlieren.

Mag auch die Spieglung im Teich
oft uns verschwimmen:
Wisse das Bild.

Erst in dem Doppelbereich
werden die Stimmen
ewig und mild.

1:9

First lift the lyre on high,
by shades surrounded.
That never-ending acclaim,
then you may sound it.

First with the dead you must eat
of their own poppies,
never again to lose even
slightest of sounds.

Though the pool's mirror may show
blurring reflections,
know the true image!

Not till the two worlds are one
will voices grow
gentle, eternal.

1:10

Euch, die ihr nie mein Gefühl verliesst,
grüss ich, antikische Sarkophage,
die das fröhliche Wasser römischer Tage
als ein wandelndes Lied durchfliesst.

Oder jene so offenen, wie das Aug
eines frohen erwachenden Hirten,
– innen voll Stille und Bienensaug –
denen entzückte Falter entschwirrten;

alle, die man dem Zweifel entreisst,
grüss ich, die wiedergeöffneten Munde,
die schon wussten, was Schweigen heisst.

Wissen wirs, Freunde, wissen wirs nicht?
beides bildet die zögernde Stunde
in dem menschlichen Angesicht.

1:10

To you who have never been far from my heart,
ancient sarcophagi, I send my greetings.
The water of Roman days runs through you, still,
a cheerful, meandering song.

Or those so wide open, like the eye
of a joyful, awakening shepherd,
stillness and bee-suck nettle within,
from which delighted butterflies flitted;

All who are being wrested from doubt,
I greet them; I greet the reopened mouths,
already acquainted with silence.

Friends, don't we know this? Do we, or not?
Both are formed by the lingering hour
on the human countenance.

1:11

Sieh den Himmel. Heisst kein Sternbild "Reiter"?
Denn dies ist uns seltsam eingeprägt:
dieser Stolz aus Erde. Und ein zweiter,
der ihn treibt und hält und den er trägt.

Ist nicht so, gejagt und dann gebändigt,
diese sehnige Natur des Seins?
Weg und Wendung. Doch ein Druck verständigt.
Neue Weite. Und die zwei sind eins.

Aber *sind* sie's? Oder meinen beide
nicht den Weg, den sie zusammen tun?
Namenlos schon trennt sie Tisch und Weide.

Auch die sternische Verbindung trügt.
Doch uns freue eine Weile nun
der Figur zu glauben. Das genügt.

1:11

Scan the heavens. Where's the constellation
that's called "horseman"? Strangely we're imprinted
with this pride of earth. And there's another,
urging, checking it, and carried by it.

Isn't our own nature's sinewy being
just like this—first whipped and then reined in?
Trail and turning. Pressure does the guiding.
New expanses. And the two are one.

Are they *really*, though? Are both committed
to the road they're traveling together?
Table, pasture—gulfs apart already.

Star connections also prove deceptive.
So just let us for awhile enjoy
our belief in them. That is enough.

1:12

Heil dem Geist, der uns verbinden mag;
denn wir leben wahrhaft in Figuren.
Und mit kleinen Schritten gehn die Uhren
neben unserm eigentlichen Tag.

Ohne unsern wahren Platz zu kennen,
handeln wir aus wirklichem Bezug.
Die Antennen fühlen die Antennen,
und die leere Ferne trug...

Reine Spannung. O Musik der Kräfte!
Ist nicht durch die lässlichen Geschäfte
jede Störung von dir abgelenkt?

Selbst wenn sich der Bauer sorgt und handelt,
wo die Saat in Sommer sich verwandelt,
reicht er niemals hin. Die Erde *schenkt*.

1:12

Hail the spirit that has power to join us.
For we truly live by means of symbols.
And with little steps the clocks are running
right along beside our actual day.

Though we do not know our own true place,
deep connections guide us as we act.
Our antennae sense far-off antennae.
Empty distances transmit . . .

Oh, pure tension. Music of these forces!
Don't your casual, everyday affairs
screen you well from every interference?

All the farmer's care, and all his nurture
of the seeds transforming into summer
do not reach them. For they are earth's *gift*.

1:13

Voller Apfel, Birne und Banane,
Stachelbeere ... Alles dieses spricht
Tod und Leben in den Mund ... Ich ahne ...
Lest es einem Kind vom Angesicht,

wenn es sie erschmeckt. Dies kommt von weit.
Wird euch langsam namenlos im Munde?
Wo sonst Worte waren, fliessen Funde,
von dem Fruchtfleisch überrascht befreit.

Wagt zu sagen, was ihr Apfel nennt.
Diese Süsse, die sich erst verdichtet,
um, im Schmecken leise aufgerichtet,

klar zu werden, wach und transparent,
doppeldeutig, sonnig, erdig, hiesig –:
O Erfahrung, Fühlung, Freude –, riesig!

1:13

Full, round apple, yellow pear, banana,
gooseberry . . . they speak of life and death
in the mouth. And, ah! Such intimations!
You can read them on the children's faces

as they taste them. This comes from afar.
Does your mouth feel gradually nameless?
In the place of words, discoveries flow,
startled to be freed of their fruit's substance.

Dare to tell me what you mean by apple.
Sweetness that begins by growing denser,
gently rising up as it is tasted,

then becoming clear, awake, transparent,
all ambiguous, sunny, earthy, earthly.
Ah, to sense, to savor, to enjoy—tremendous!

1:14

Wir gehen um mit Blume, Weinblatt, Frucht.
Sie sprechen nicht die Sprache nur des Jahres.
Aus Dunkel steigt ein buntes Offenbares
und hat vielleicht den Glanz der Eifersucht

der Toten an sich, die die Erde stärken.
Was wissen wir von ihrem Teil an dem?
Es ist seit lange ihre Art, den Lehm
mit ihrem freien Marke zu durchmärken.

Nun fragt sich nur: tun sie es gern? . . .
Drängt diese Frucht, ein Werk von schweren Sklaven
geballt zu uns empor, zu ihren Herrn?

Sind *sie* die Herrn, die bei den Wurzeln schlafen,
und gönnen uns aus ihren Überflüssen
dies Zwischending aus stummer Kraft und Küssen?

1:14

We grow and care for flower, grape leaf, fruit.
They don't just speak the language of the year.
Colorful forms are rising from the dark
wearing, perhaps, the glint of jealousy

that the earth nurturers—the dead—might feel.
What do we know about their part in this?
It's been their custom for these many years
to nurture our loam with their freed marrow.

But now the question is, do they enjoy it?
Or is this fruit, produced by heavy slaves,
offered to us, their masters, like a fist?

Are *they* the masters, sleeping by the roots,
merely bequeathing us out of their bounty
ambiguous harvests, half mute strength, half kisses?

1:15

Wartet . . . , das schmeckt . . . Schon ists auf der Flucht.
. . . Wenig Musik nur, ein Stampfen, ein Summen –:
Mädchen, ihr warmen, Mädchen, ihr stummen,
tanzt den Geschmack der erfahrenen Frucht!

Tanzt die Orange. Wer kann sie vergessen,
wie sie, ertrinkend in sich, sich wehrt
wider ihr Süss-sein. Ihr habt sie besessen.
Sie hat sich köstlich zu euch bekehrt.

Tanzt die Orange. Die wärmere Landschaft,
werft sie aus euch, dass die reife erstrahle
in Lüften der Heimat! Erglühte, enthüllt

Düfte um Düfte! Schafft die Verwandschaft
mit der reinen, sich weigernden Schale,
mt dem Saft, der die Glückliche füllt!

1:15

Wait . . . oh, what flavor . . . already escaping.
A bit of soft music, some stamping, some humming:
You silent young girls—girls heated with dancing—
dance the taste of the fruit you have known!

Yes, dance the orange, for who can forget it,
as, in itself drowning, it struggles against its
own orange-sweetness. You have possessed it.
Deliciously it has converted to you.

Dance it—the orange. That balmier landscape,
spread it around you. The native land's breezes,
let them enkindle it! Glowing ones, show to us

fragrance on fragrance! Create our connection
with its pure and reluctant rind, with the
juices that fill this fruit of delight!

1:16

Du, mein Freund, bist einsam, weil . . .
Wir machen mit Worten und Fingerzeigen
uns allmählich die Welt zu eigen,
vielleicht ihren schwächsten, gefährlichsten Teil.

Wer zeigt mit Fingern auf einen Geruch? –
Doch von den Kräften, die uns bedrohten,
fühlst du viele. .. Du kennst die Toten,
und du erschrickst vor dem Zauberspruch.

Sieh, nun heisst es, zusammen ertragen
Stückwerk und Teile, als sei es das Ganze.
Dir helfen, wird schwer sein. Vor allem: pflanze

mich nicht in dein Herz. Ich wüchse zu schnell.
Doch *meines* Herrn Hand will ich führen und sagen:
Hier. Das ist Esau in seinem Fell.

1:16

You, my friend, are lonely. That's because . . .
Speaking words and pointing with fingers,
we make the world our own by and by,
perhaps its weakest, most dangerous part.

An odor, though—who'd point a finger at that?
Yet of the menacing powers that beset us,
You feel many . . . Aware of the dead,
you are frightened away by the magic spell.

Now, you see, we must bear them together,
the fragments and pieces, as if they were one.
Hard to help you. Above all, don't plant

me in your heart. I would grow too fast.
But I will guide *my* master's hand and tell him,
"Here—this is Esau beneath his pelt."

1:17

Zu unterst der Alte, verworrn,
all der Erbauten
Wurzel, verborgener Born,
den sie nie schauten.

Sturmhelm und Jägerhorn,
Spruch von Ergrauten,
Männer im Brüderzorn,
Frauen wie Lauten . . .

Drängender Zweig an Zweig,
nirgends ein freier . . .
Einer! o steig . . . o steig . . .

Aber sie brechen noch.
Dieser erst oben doch
biegt sich zur Leier.

1:17

At bottom, the Old One, a tangle,
all the whole structure's
root, hidden wellspring below.
They never saw him.

Helmet and hunting horn,
sayings of graybeards,
Brothers in anger met,
women like lutes . . .

Branch closely crowds on branch,
never a free one...
Yes—there is one! Climb on!

Yet they are breaking still.
This top one, finally,
will make a lyre.

1:18

Hörst du das Neue, Herr,
dröhnen und beben?
Kommen Verkündiger,
die es erheben.

Zwar ist kein Hören heil
in dem Durchtobtsein,
doch der Maschinenteil
will jetzt gelobt sein.

Sieh, die Maschine:
wie sie sich wälzt und rächt
und uns entstellt und schwächt.

Hat sie aus uns auch Kraft,
sie, ohne Leidenschaft
treibe und diene.

1:18

Master—hear that new sound,
booming, vibrating?
Prophets come praising it,
come to exalt it.

Though we are deafened by
this noise and furor,
still, the machine is here;
it demands homage.

Look, the machine: It is
wallowing in vengeance. It
weakens, disfigures us.

It draws its strength from us,
so, without passion, it
should work and serve us.

1:19

Wandelt sich rasch auch die Welt
wie Wolkengestalten,
alles Vollendete fällt
heim zum Uralten.

Über dem Wandel und Gang,
weiter und freier,
währt noch dein Vor-Gesang,
Gott mit der Leier.

Nicht sind die Leiden erkannt,
nicht ist die Liebe gelernt,
und was im Tod uns entfernt,

ist nicht entschleiert.
Einzig das Lied überm Land
heiligt und feiert.

1:19

Though the world rapidly changes—
cloud figures passing,
all that's perfected returns
home to Beginnings.

Over this movement and flow,
farther and freer,
still lasts your primal song,
god of the lyre.

Suffering is still not explained,
nor have we learned how to love,
and what removes us in death—

still not revealed.
Only the song from above
celebrates, hallows.

1:20

Dir aber, Herr, o was weih ich dir, sag,
der das Ohr den Geschöpfen gelehrt? –
Mein Erinnern an einen Frühlingstag,
seinen Abend, in Russland –, ein Pferd . . .

Herüber vom Dorf kam der Schimmel allein,
an der vorderen Fessel den Pflock,
um die Nacht auf den Wiesen allein zu sein;
wie schlug seiner Mähne Gelock

an den Hals im Takte des Übermuts,
bei dem grob gehemmten Galopp.
Wie sprangen die Quellen des Rossebluts!

Der fühlte die Weiten, und ob!
Der sang und der hörte –, dein Sagenkreis
war *in* ihm geschlossen.
Sein Bild: ich weih's.

1:20

What can I consecrate, Master, to you
who taught all creation to listen?
My memory of a day in spring,
his evening, in Russia—a horse . . .

The gray came out of the village alone,
around his front fetlock a tether,
to be by himself in the fields that night;
And oh! The beat of his curly mane

on his neck, to the spirited rhythm
of that rough, that tether-obstructed gait.
How the springs of horse blood bubbled!

He felt the call of the distance—and how!
He sang and he listened. Your mythic ring—
was closed *within* him.
His image: my gift.

1:21

Frühling ist wiedergekommen. Die Erde
ist wie ein Kind, das Gedichte weiss;
viele, o viele . . . Für die Beschwerde
langen Lernens bekommt sie den Preis.

Streng war ihr Lehrer. Wir mochten das Weisse
an dem Barte des alten Manns.
Nun, wie das Grüne, das Blaue heisse,
dürfen wir fragen: sie kanns, sie kanns!

Erde, die frei hat, du glückliche, spiele
nun mit den Kindern. Wir wollen dich fangen,
fröhliche Erde. Dem Frohsten gelingst.

O, was der Lehrer sie lehrte, das Viele,
und was gedruckt steht in Wurzeln und langen
schwierigen Stämmen: sie singts, sie singts!

1:21

Spring has returned at last. The earth
is like a child who knows poems by heart,
many, oh, many! After the trouble
of hours of learning, she gets the prize.

Her teacher was strict. We liked the white hair
all through the gray of the old man's beard.
Now we may ask her the names of the colors—
the blue and the green—she knows them, she knows!

School is out, Earth! How lucky you are!
Play with the children. We'll chase you and catch you,
oh, happy Earth. And the happiest child wins.

All those things that she learned from her teacher,
all that is printed in roots and long,
difficult tree trunks: She sings it, she sings!

1:22

Wir sind die Treibenden.
Aber den Schritt der Zeit,
nehmt ihn als Kleinigkeit
im immer Bleibenden.

Alles das Eilende
wird schon vorüber sein;
denn das Verweilende
erst weiht uns ein.

Knaben, o, werft den Mut
nicht in die Schnelligkeit,
nicht in den Flugversuch.

Alles ist ausgeruht:
Dunkel und Helligkeit,
Blume und Buch.

1:22

We are the driving ones.
Yet, the way time goes by—
see that as trivial,
next to what stays.

All that is rushing by,
will be long over soon;
only what then remains
consecrates us.

Youths, do not throw yourselves
into mere speed alone,
into attempted flight.

All is at peace, at rest:
darkness and light,
blossom and book.

1:23

O, erst *dann*, wenn der Flug
nicht mehr um seinetwillen
wird in die Himmelsstillen
steigen, sich selbst genug,

um, in lichten Profilen,
als das Gerät, das gelang,
Liebling der Winde zu spielen,
sicher, schwenkend, und schlank, –

erst, wenn ein reines Wohin
wachsender Apparate
Knabenstolz überwiegt

wird, überstürzt von Gewinn
jener den Fernen Genahte
sein, was er einsam erfliegt.

1:23

Oh, it is *only* when flight
no longer for its own sake
climbs to the silent heavens,
its own beginning and end,

in mere display of bright profiles,
as the successful device,
favored by every wind,
confident, swaying, and slim—no,

not till the pure goal alone wins
out over all boyish pride
in growing flying machines,

will, overtaken by gain,
those who came from afar
be what their lonely flight sought.

1:24

Sollen wir unsere uralte Freundschaft, die grossen
niemals werbenden Götter, weil sie der harte
Stahl, den wir streng erzogen, nicht kennt, verstossen
oder sie plötzlich suchen auf einer Karte?

Diese gewaltigen Freunde, die uns die Toten
nehmen, rühren nirgends an unsere Räder.
Unsere Gastmähler haben wir weit –, unsere Bäder
Fortgerückt, und ihre uns lang schon zu langsamen Boten

überholen wir immer. Einsamer nun auf einander
ganz angewiesen, ohne einander zu kennen,
führen wir nicht mehr die Pfade als schöne Mäander

sondern als Grade. Nur noch in Dampfkesseln brennen
die einstigen Feuer und heben die Hämmer, die immer
grössern. Wir aber nehmen an Kraft ab, wie Schwimmer.

1:24

Should we be banishing our age-old friendship, the great
gods never-wooing, because the hard steel
that we so strictly reared has no knowledge of them?
Or should we suddenly search for them on a map?

These, the powerful friends who take our dead from us
are no longer touching our wheels anywhere.
Our banquets we've moved, and our baths, far away,
and their messengers, long much too slow for us—

we're always passing them. Lonelier now, we are
wholly dependent on one another, though strangers.
We no longer make lovely meandering paths.

No—we make straight ones. Our former fires are burning
only in steam boilers now; they are lifting their hammers,
ever larger ones, while we lose strength, like swimmers.

1:25

Dich aber will ich nun, *dich*, die ich kannte
wie eine Blume, von der ich den Namen nicht weiss,
noch *ein* Mal erinnern und ihnen zeigen, Entwandte,
schöne Gespielin des unüberwindlichen Schrei's.

Tänzerin erst, die plötzlich, den Körper voll Zögern,
anhielt, als göss man ihr Jungsein in Erz;
trauernd und lauschend –. Da, von den hohen Vermögern
fiel ihr Musik in das veränderte Herz.

Nah war die Krankheit. Schon von den Schatten bemächtigt,
drängte verdunkelt das Blut, doch, wie flüchtig verdächtigt,
trieb es in seinen natürlichen Frühling hervor.

Wieder und wieder, von Dunkel und Sturz unterbrochen,
glänzte es irdisch. Bis es nach schrecklichem Pochen
trat in das trostlos offene Tor.

1:25

You, though, I'm longing, *you*, whom I knew
like a blossom whose name I cannot recall,
to remember *once more*, and show them, stolen one,
beautiful playmate of the unquellable scream.

A dancer at first, who slowed and suddenly stopped,
as if her young limbs were filling with iron,
mournfully listening, till, sent by high powers,
music descended, filling her altered heart.

Sickness was near. Already empowered by shadows,
her darkened blood surged, yet, as if briefly suspected,
flowed out, finally, into its natural springtime.

Time after time, interrupted by darkness and falling,
it showed an earthly sheen until, after terrible knocking,
it stepped through the desolate open gate.

1:26

Du aber, Göttlicher, du, bis zuletzt noch Ertöner,
da ihn der Schwarm der verschmähten Mänaden befiel,
hast ihr Geschrei übertönt mit Ordnung, du Schöner,
aus den Zerstörenden stieg dein erbauendes Spiel.

Keine war da, dass sie Haupt dir und Leier zerstör.
Wie sie auch rangen und rasten, und alle die scharfen
Steine, die sie nach deinem Herzen warfen,
wurden zu Sanftem an dir und begabt mit Gehör.

Schliesslich zerschlugen sie dich, von der Rache gehetzt,
während dein Klang noch in Löwen und Felsen verweilte
und in den Bäumen und Vögeln. Dort singst du noch jetzt.

O du verlorener Gott! Du unendliche Spur!
Nur weil dich reissend zuletzt die Feindschaft verteilte,
sind wir die Hörenden jetzt und ein Mund der Natur.

1:26

You, divine singer, whose singing endured to the end,
when he was attacked by that swarm of rejected maenads—
you drowned their shrieks with harmony, beautiful singer.
From their destruction rose your inspiring song.

None of the lot could destroy your head or your lyre,
although they wrestled and raged, and the sharpness
of all those stones they hurled at your heart
turned into gentleness gifted with hearing.

Driven by vengeance, they finally broke you apart,
while your sound still lingered in lions and boulders,
and in the trees and the birds. You are singing there, still.

Oh, you lost god! Track whose ending we'll never discover!
Only because your enemies tore you apart
we are the hearers now, one of nature's mouths.

2:1

Atmen, du unsichtbares Gedicht!
Immerfort um das eigne
Sein rein eingetauschter Weltraum. Gegengewicht,
in dem ich mich rhythmisch ereigne.

Einzige Welle, deren
allmähliches Meer ich bin;
sparsamstes du von allen möglichen Meeren, –
Raumgewinn.

Wieviele von diesen Stellen der Räume waren schon
innen in mir. Manche Winde
sind wie mein Sohn.

Erkennst du mich, Luft, du, voll noch einst meiniger Orte?
Du, einmal glatte Rinde,
Rundung und Blatt meiner Worte.

2:1

Breathing—you invisible poem!
Outer space, continually
exchanged for my own pure being. Counterweight,
site of my rhythmical realization.

Single wave of which
I am the gradual sea;
you are the most frugal of all possible seas—
space to be gained.

How many of these portions of space were once
inside of me. Some of the winds
are like my son.

Do you remember me, air, still full of my former places?
You were once the smooth bark,
the curve and leaf of my words.

2:2

So wie dem Meister manchmal das eilig
nähere Blatt den *wirklichen* Strich
abnimmt: so nehmen oft Spiegel das heilig
einzige Lächeln der Mädchen in sich,

wenn sie den Morgen erproben, allein, –
oder im Glanze der dienenden Lichter.
Und in das Atmen der echten Gesichter,
später, fällt nur ein Widerschein.

Was haben Augen einst ins umrusste
lange Verglühn der Kamine geschaut:
Blicke des Lebens, für immer verlorne.

Ach, der Erde, wer kennt die Verluste?
Nur, wer mit dennoch preisendem Laut
sänge das Herz, das ins Ganze geborne.

2:2

Just as the paper that chanced to be near
sometimes the master's *true* line will claim,
mirrors often absorb the young girls'
holy, never-repeated smiles,

when they are testing the morning, alone,
or by the light of the candles that serve them.
The breathing, actual faces, later
only receive reflected smiles.

How did eyes stare, in times past, at the soot-framed,
gradual, fading glow of their fires!
Glimpses of life that we've lost forever.

Ah! The earth's losses—who fathoms them all?
Only those who sing in spite of them,
praising the heart that was born into wholeness.

2:3

Spiegel: noch nie hat man wissend beschrieben,
was ihr in euerem Wesen seid.
Ihr, wie mit lauter Löchern von Sieben
erfüllten Zwischenräume der Zeit.

Ihr, noch des leeren Saales Verschwender –,
wenn es dämmert, wie Wälder weit . . .
Und der Lüster geht wie ein Sechzehn-Ender
durch eure Unbetretbarkeit.

Manchmal seid ihr voll Malerei.
Einige scheinen *in* euch gegangen –,
andere schicktet ihre scheu vorbei.

Aber die Schönste wird bleiben –, bis
drüben in ihre enthaltenen Wangen
eindrang der klare, gelöste Narziss.

2:3

Mirrors: There's never been true description
of what, in your innermost nature, you are.
You, who seem made of the holes of sieves
filled with the in-between spaces of time.

You, who waste even the empty ballroom—
when dusk is falling, like forests wide . . .
and the chandelier strides like a sixteen-point buck
straight through your impenetrability.

At times we see you filled with paintings.
Certain ones seem to have *entered* you;
others you've bashfully sent on their way.

The loveliest, though, will remain, until
radiant Narcissus has penetrated
her modest, maidenly cheeks below.

2:4

O dieses ist das Tier, das es nicht giebt.
Sie wusstens nicht und habens jeden Falls
– sein Wandeln, seine Haltung, seinen Hals,
bis in des stillen Blickes Licht – geliebt.

Zwar *war* es nicht. Doch weil sie's liebten, ward
ein reines Tier. Sie liessen immer Raum.
Und in dem Raume, klar und ausgespart,
erhob es leicht sein Haupt und brauchte kaum

zu sein. Sie nährten es mit keinem Korn,
nur immer mit der Möglichkeit, es sei.
Und die gab solche Stärke an das Tier,

dass es aus sich heraus ein Stirnhorn trieb. Ein Horn.
Zu einer Jungfrau kam es weiss herbei –
und war im Silber-Spiegel und in ihr.

2:4

This is the non-existent beast. They did
not know that it did not exist and so
they loved it anyway—gait, posture, crest,
down to the very gaze of its still eyes.

True, it did *not* exist, but since they loved it,
a pure beast came to be. They always gave it space,
and in that clear, bright space they saved for it,
it raised its head a little, scarcely needing

to be. They did not nourish it with grain,
just with the possibility of being.
And that endowed the beast with such great strength

it grew a frontal horn. A unicorn.
When, in its whiteness, it approached a virgin,
it *was*, within the mirror, within her.

2:5

Blumenmuskel, der der Anemone
Wiesenmorgen nach und nach erschliesst,
bis in ihren Schooss das polyphone
Licht der lauten Himmel sich ergiesst,

in den stillen Blütenstern gespannter
Muskel des unendlichen Empfangs,
manchmal *so* von Fülle übermannter,
dass der Ruhewink des Untergangs

kaum vermag die weitzurückgeschnellten
Blätterränder dir zurückzugeben:
du, Entschluss und Kraft von *wie*viel Welten!

Wir, Gewaltsamen, wir währen länger.
Aber *wann*, in welchem aller Leben,
sind wir endlich offen und Empfänger?

2:5

Flower muscle, gradually disclosing
meadow morning to the anemone,
until loud skies' polyphonic light,
pours into her opening womb,

infinite conception's muscle,
stretched within this still, small flower star,
sometimes overwhelmed by fullness
so completely, that the beckoning

peace of dissolution's barely able
to return your wide-flung petal edges:
You—resolve and power of *countless* worlds!

We, the violent ones, we last much longer.
Ah, but *when*, in which of all our lives will
we at last be open to conception?

2:6

Rose, du thronende, denen im Altertume
warst du ein Kelch mit einfachem Rand.
Uns aber bist du die volle zahllose Blume,
der unerschöpfliche Gegenstand.

In deinem Reichtum scheinst du wie Kleidung um Kleidung
um einen Leib aus nichts als Glanz;
aber dein einzelnes Blatt ist zugleich die Vermeidung
und die Verleugnung jedes Gewands.

Seit Jahrhunderten ruft uns dein Duft
seine süssesten Namen herüber;
plötzlich liegt er wie Ruhm in der Luft.

Dennoch, wir wissen ihn nicht zu nennen, wir raten . . .
Und Erinnerung geht zu ihm über,
die wir von rufbaren Stunden erbaten.

2:6

Rose on your throne—you were to the ancients
a goblet, a calyx with simple edge.
To *us* you are the filled, the numberless blossom,
the object that's inexhaustible.

In your wealth you wear layers on layers of dresses
surrounding a body of nothing but light. Yet
each of the petals becomes, at the same time,
avoidance as well as denial of any dress.

For centuries now, your fragrance has called
over to us the sweetest of names.
It suddenly fills the air like fame.

Still, we do not know what to call it; we're guessing . . .
and we send memories out to meet it,
requested from hours that would come to our call.

2:7

Blumen, ihr schliesslich den ordnenden Händen verwandte,
(Händen der Mädchen von einst und jetzt)
die auf dem Gartentisch oft von Kante zu Kante
lagen, ermattet und sanft verletzt,

wartend des Wassers, das sie noch einmal erhole
aus dem begonnenen Tod –, und nun
wieder erhobene zwischen die strömende Pole
fühlender Finger, die wohlzutun

mehr noch vermögen, als ihr ahnet, ihr leichten,
wenn ihr euch wiederfandet im Krug,
langsam erkühlend und Warmes der Mädchen, wie Beichten,

von euch gebend, wie trübe ermüdende Sünden,
die das Gepflücktsein beging, als Bezug
wieder zu ihnen, die sich euch blühend verbünden.

2:7

Flowers, you ultimate kin to the hands that arrange you,
(hands of the girls of yesterday and today)
often lying across the garden table
feeling exhausted and slightly hurt,

waiting for water to bring them back once more
from the beginning of death, and now
raised up again between streaming poles
of sensitive fingers, whose healing touch

helps much more than you thought it would, delicate flowers,
when you found yourselves placed in a jug,
slowly cooling, releasing the warmth of the girls—

dreary, dispiriting sins, that being picked
committed on you to renew once more
the connection with those who are blooming like you.

2:8

Wenige ihr, der einstigen Kindheit Gespielen
in den zerstreuten Gärten der Stadt:
wie wir uns fanden und uns zögernd gefielen
und, wie das Lamm mit dem redenden Blatt,

sprachen als Schweigende. Wenn wir uns einmal freuten,
keinem gehörte es. Wessen wars?
Und wie zergings unten allen den gehenden Leuten
und im Bangen des langen Jahrs.

Wagen umrollten uns fremd, vorübergezogen,
Häuser umstanden uns stark, aber unwahr, – und keines
kannte uns je. *Was* war wirklich im All?

Nichts. Nur die Bälle. Ihre herrlichen Bogen.
Auch nicht die Kinder . . . aber manchmal trat eines,
Ach ein vergehendes, unter den fallenden Ball.

In memoriam Egon von Rilke.

2:8

Few you were, my long-ago childhood's playmates,
in the scattered gardens of town;
how we discovered and shyly befriended each other,
and, like the lamb with the talking scroll

spoke through our silence. Our occasional joy—
none of us owned it. Whose, then, was it?
And how it melted away under passing feet,
and in the cares of the endless year.

Alien carriages rolled all around us and passed us.
The houses surrounding us were strong, but unreal. And none,
none ever knew us. *What,* in our world, was real?

Nothing. Only the balls. Their wonderful arcs.
Nor were the children . . . But sometimes one of them stepped,
ah, a mortal one, under the falling ball.

In memoriam Egon von Rilke

2:9

Rühmt euch, ihr Richtenden, nicht der entbehrlichen Folter
und dass das Eisen nicht länger an Hälsen sperrt.
Keins ist gesteigert, kein Herz –, weil ein gewollter
Krampf der Milde euch zarter verzerrt.

Was es durch Zeiten bekam, das schenkt das Schafott
wieder zurück, wie Kinder ihr Spielzeug vom vorig
alten Geburtstag. Ins reine, ins hohe, ins thorig
offene Herz träte er anders, der Gott

wirklicher Milde. Er käme gewaltig und griffe
strahlender um sich, wie Göttliche sind.
Mehr als ein Wind für die grossen gesicherten Schiffe.

Weniger nicht, als die heimlich leise Gewahrung,
die uns im Innern schweigend gewinnt
wie ein still spielendes Kind aus unendlicher Paarung.

2:9

Judges—you should not be boasting of optional torture
and of the necks no longer encircled by chains.
No heart is heightened—not one—by the deliberate
spasm of mildness more mildly disfiguring you.

All that the ages gave it, the guillotine renders
back, as children return their last birthday's playthings.
Into the pure, the high, the gate-open heart, he would
enter a different way, the god of genuine

mildness; he'd come with great might and reach out
in greater radiance, as the divine ones do.
More than a wind for the ships that are large and secure,

but never less than the secret, still realization,
which, without words, deep inside, wins us over—
a quietly playing child, fruit of endless embrace.

2:10

Alles Erworbne bedroht die Maschine, solange
sie sich erdreistet, im Geist, statt im Gehorchen zu sein.
Dass nicht der herrlichen Hand schöneres Zögern mehr prange
zu dem entschlossenern Bau schneidet sie steifer den Stein.

Nirgends bleibt sie zurück, dass wir ihr *ein* Mal entrönnen
und sie in stiller Fabrik ölend sich selber gehört.
Sie ist das Leben, – sie meint es am besten zu können,
die mit dem gleichen Entschluss ordnet und schafft
        und zerstört.

Aber noch ist unser Dasein verzaubert; an hundert
Stellen ist es noch Ursprung. Ein Spielen von reinen
Kräften, die keiner berührt, der nicht kniet und bewundert.

Worte gehen noch zart am Unsäglichen aus . . .
Und die Musik, immer neu, aus den bebendsten Steinen,
baut im unbrauchbaren Raum ihr vergöttlichtes Haus.

2:10

All we've attained the machine will threaten, as long
as it seeks brashly to be spirit instead of obedience.
So that the marvelous hand's lovelier lingering might not
    outshine it,
It cuts more stiffly the more resolute building's stone.

It never falls behind, so we might at least *once* escape,
leaving it in the empty factory, oiling itself, alone.
No—the machine is life, and is sure it does everything best,
in one and the same resolve designing, creating, destroying.

Yet, still our lives are enchanted. A hundred places are
fresh and original, still. There, pure powers play
touched by no one who does not kneel and admire.

Words still fade gently away before the unsayable . . .
Music, in endless renewal, from the most quivering stones
builds in unusable space its deified house.

2:11

Manche, des Todes, entstand ruhig geordnete Regel,
weiterbezwingender Mensch, seit du im Jagen beharrst;
mehr doch als Falle und Netz weiss ich dich, Streifen von Segel,
den man hinuntergehängt in den höhligen Karst.

Leise liess man dich ein, als wärst du ein Zeichen,
Frieden zu feiern. Doch dann: rang dich am Rande der Knecht,
—und, aus den Höhlen, die Nacht warf eine Handvoll
        von bleichen
taumelnden Tauben ins Licht ...
                        Aber auch *das* ist im Recht.

Fern von dem Schauenden sei jeglicher Hauch des Bedauerns,
nicht nur vom Jäger allein, der, was sich zeitig erweist,
wachsam und handelnd vollzieht.

Töten ist eine Gestalt unseres wandernden Trauerns ...
Rein ist im heiteren Geist,
was an uns selber geschieht.

2:11

Many a calmly-composed usage of death has evolved,
ever-conquering man, since you have persisted in hunting.
Better than trap and net, I know you, oh, strip of sailcloth,
hanging far down the cavernous limestone cliff.

Gently they lowered you; you seemed a signal to celebrate
peace. But then: The hired man twisted you, holding your edge.
And the night, from out of the cave hurled a handful of pale
tumbling doves into the light . . .
                    but *this, too*, is right.

Far from the observer be even the breath of regret,
not just from the hunter, who, watchful and active,
achieves what needs to be done.

Killing is just one form of our nomadic mourning.
a spirit serene renders pure
whatever may happen to us.

2:12

Wolle die Wandlung. O sei für die Flamme begeistert,
drin sich ein Ding dir entzieht, das mit Verwandlungen prunkt;
jener entwerfende Geist, welcher das Irdische meistert,
liebt in dem Schwung der Figur nichts wie den
      wendenden Punkt.

Was sich ins Bleiben verschliesst, schon *ists* das Erstarrte;
Wähnt es sich sicher im Schutz des unscheinbaren Grau's?
Warte, ein Härtestes warnt aus der Ferne das Harte.
Wehe –: abwesender Hammer holt aus!

Wer sich als Quelle ergiesst, den erkennt die Erkennung;
und sie führt ihn entzückt durch das heiter Geschaffne,
das mit Anfang oft schliesst und mit Ende beginnt.

Jeder glückliche Raum ist Kind oder Enkel von Trennung,
den sie staunend durchgehn. Und die verwandelte Daphne
will, seit sie lorbeern fühlt, dass du dich wandelst in Wind.

2:12

Trust transformation. Oh, thrill to the glow of the flame
veiling a thing that eludes you while flaunting its changings.
For the creative spirit that masters all earthly things
loves in the flow of the figure only its pivoting point.

Locked into permanence, all is frozen already.
Is there safety, then, in inconspicuous gray?
Wait! The hardest of all gives warning to hardness.
Oh, look out! A faraway hammer is raised.

Those who pour themselves out like a stream are
    acknowledged by knowledge,
and in delight she leads them through her serene creation,
which with beginnings often concludes, to begin with the end.

Each radiant space is the child or grandchild of separation,
and in amazement they cross it. Daphne transformed
utters a laurel tree's wish that you might transform into wind.

2:13

Sei allem Abschied voran, als wäre er hinter
dir, wie der Winter, der eben geht.
Denn unter Wintern ist einer so endlos Winter,
dass, überwinternd, dein Herz überhaupt übersteht.

Sei immer tot in Euridike –, singender steige,
preisender steige zurück in den reinen Bezug.
Hier, unter Schwindenden, sei, im Reiche der Neige,
sei ein klingendes Glas, das sich im Klang schon zerschlug.

Sei – und wisse zugleich des Nicht-Seins Bedingung,
den unendlichen Grund deiner innigen Schwingung,
dass du sie völlig vollziehst dieses einzige Mal.

Zu dem gebrauchten, sowohl wie zum dumpfen und stummen
Vorrat der vollen Natur, den unsäglichen Summen,
zähle dich jubelnd hinzu und vernichte die Zahl.

2:13

Be ahead of all parting, as if it were
behind you like the winter just passing now.
For among winters there's one such endless winter,
that, overwintering, your heart for all time overcomes.

Always be dead in Eurydice; with stronger song,
giving more powerful praise, re-ascend to pure relation.
Here, among the vanishing ones, in the realm of decline,
be as a ringing glass, already shattered by ringing.

Be, and know at the same time the terms of non-being—
endless reason for your intense vibration,
so you may perfectly, this one time, achieve it.

Count yourself in with the used as well as the dumb, dark
stores of bountiful nature, with the unsayable sums.
Count yourself, jubilantly, and cancel the count.

2:14

Siehe die Blumen, diese dem Irdischen treuen,
denen wir Schicksal vom Rande des Schicksals leihn, –
aber wer weiss es! Wenn sie ihr Welken bereuen,
ist es an uns, ihre Reue zu sein.

Alles will schweben. Da gehn wir umher wie Beschwerer,
legen auf alles uns selbst, vom Gewichte entzückt;
o was sind wir den Dingen für zehrende Lehrer,
weil ihnen ewige Kindheit glückt.

Nähme sie einer ins innige Schlafen und schliefe
tief mit den Dingen –; o wie käme er leicht,
anders zum anderen Tag, aus der gemeinsamen Tiefe.

Oder er bliebe vielleicht, und sie blühten und priesen
ihn, den Bekehrten, der nun den Ihrigen gleicht,
allen den stillen Geschwistern im Winde der Wiesen.

2:14

Look at the flowers—they are so faithful to earth—
whom we lend fate off of the edges of fate . . .
But then, who knows! When they are regretting their wilting
we might be called on to be their regret.

All things long to be soaring, and we go around
heavily laying ourselves on them, thrilled with our weight.
Oh, what consuming teachers we're being to them,
just because they have captured eternal childhood.

If we'd enfold them in intimate sleep, sleeping
deeply with them, oh, how lightly we'd come, differently,
out of shared depths, renewed, to the new day.

Or perhaps we would stay, and they'd bloom and praise
us, their converts, resembling one of their own now—
their silent sisters blown by the meadow wind.

2:15

O Brunnen-Mund, du gebender, du Mund,
der unerschöpflich Eines, Reines spricht, –
du, vor des Wassers fliessendem Gesicht,
marmorne Maske. Und im Hintergrund

der Aquädukte Herkunft. Weither an
Gräbern vorbei, vom Hang des Apennins
tragen sie dir dein Sagen zu, das dann
am schwarzen Altern deines Kinns

vorüberfällt in das Gefäss davor.
Dies ist das schlafend hingelegte Ohr,
das Marmor-Ohr, in das du immer sprichst.

Ein Ohr der Erde. Nur mit sich allein
redet sie also. Schiebt ein Krug sich ein,
so scheint es ihr, dass du sie unterbrichst.

2:15

Oh, giving, overflowing fountain mouth,
that inexhaustibly the same pure message brings—
you are a marble mask held up before
the water's flowing face. Behind you lie

the aqueducts where you originated.
Past graves and down the sloping Apennines,
they send your sayings to you; which then flow
along the blackened aging of your chin,

into the vessel standing there before you.
This is the sleeping, the recumbent ear,
the marble ear you always speak into.

One of the earth's ears. Only with herself
she speaks, therefore. And when a jug intrudes,
it seems to her that you are interrupting.

2:16

Immer wieder von uns aufgerissen,
ist der Gott die Stelle, welche heilt.
Wir sind Scharfe, denn wir wollen wissen,
aber er ist heiter und verteilt.

Selbst die reine, die geweihte Spende
nimmt er anders nicht in seine Welt,
als indem er sich dem freien Ende
unbewegt entgegenstellt.

Nur der Tote trinkt
aus der hier von uns *gehörten* Quelle,
wenn der Gott ihm schweigend winkt, dem Toten.

Uns wird nur der Lärm geboten.
Und das Lamm erbittet seine Schelle
aus dem stilleren Instinkt.

2:16

When we tear it open, every time, we
tear the god who tries to heal our injury.
We're the sharp ones, for we want to know.
But he is diffuse serenity.

Even pure and consecrated offerings
he receives into his world no way but this:
stands and faces them—their unheld end—
simply waiting, motionless.

Only dead men drink
from the spring we only *hear,* and when,
wordlessly, the god invites them to.

We are only offered noise.
And the lamb requests its bell
prompted by a quieter instinct.

2:17

Wo, in welchen immer selig bewässerten Gärten, an welchen
Bäumen, aus welchen zärtlich entblätterten Blüten-Kelchen
reifen die fremdartigen Früchte der Tröstung? Diese
köstlichen, deren du eine vielleicht in der zertretenen Wiese

deiner Armut findest. Von einem zum anderen Male
wunderst du dich über die Grösse der Frucht,
über ihr Heilsein, über die Sanftheit der Schale,
und dass der Leichtsinn des Vogels dir nicht vorwegnahm
        und nicht die Eifersucht

unten des Wurms. Gibt es denn Bäume, von Engeln beflogen,
und von verborgenen langsamen Gärtnern so seltsam gezogen
dass sie uns tragen, ohne uns zu gehören?

Haben wir niemals vermocht, wir Schatten und Schemen,
durch unser voreilig reifes und wieder welkes Benehmen
jener gelassenen Sommer Gleichmut zu stören?

2:17

Where, in which orchards, always blissfully watered, and on
which trees, from which tenderly stripped flower calyxes
do the exotic fruits of our consolation ripen? These
    delicious ones,
one of which you might find on the trampled field

of your poverty. Over and over again,
you are amazed at the size of the fruit,
that it's unblemished, and has such a gentle rind,
and that the careless bird did not get it before you,
    nor the covetous

worm down below. Are there really, then, trees,
    pollinated by angels,
and so remarkably tended by slow, hidden gardeners
that they are able to bear for us though they're not ours?

Have we never been able, we shades and abstractions,
through our premature ripening or, again, wilting behavior
to mar the peace and serenity of those summers?

2:18

Tänzerin: o du Verlegung
alles Vergehens in Gang: wie brachtest du's dar.
Und der Wirbel am Schluss, dieser Baum aus Bewegung,
nahm er nicht ganz in Besitz das erschwungene Jahr?

Blühte nicht, dass ihn dein Schwingen von vorhin umschwärme
plötzlich sein Wipfel aus Stille? Und über ihr,
war sie nicht Sonne, war sie nicht Sommer, die Wärme,
diese unzählige Wärme aus dir?

Aber er trug auch, er trug, dein Baum der Ekstase.
Sind sie nicht seine ruhigen Früchte: der Krug,
reifend gestreift, und die gereiftere Vase?

Und in den Bildern: ist nicht die Zeichnung geblieben,
die deiner Braue dunkler Zug
rasch an die Wandung der eigenen Wendung geschrieben?

2:18

Dancer: You are transference
of all that passes to passage. Oh, you presented it well.
And that final whirling, that tree made of motion,
didn't it fully possess the spiraling year?

Wasn't its crown of stillness suddenly blooming,
the better to feel you, whirling about its leaves?
And above her, the warmth—wasn't it sun, wasn't it summer,
that countless warmth that was coming from you?

But it also bore fruit—yes, your tree of ecstasy bore.
For aren't these its tranquil fruits: the jug,
ripened in stripes, and the vase that is even riper?

And in the images: didn't the line remain
made by your eyebrow's dark stroke,
hastily scratched on the wall of your own winding turn?

2:19

Irgendwo wohnt das Gold in der verwöhnenden Bank
und mit Tausenden tut es vertraulich. Doch jener
Blinde, der Bettler, ist selbst dem kupfernen Zehner
wie ein verlorener Ort, wie das staubige Eck unterm Schrank.

In den Geschäften entlang ist das Gold wie zuhause
und verkleidet sich scheinbar in Seide, Nelken und Pelz.
Er, der Schweigende, steht in der Atempause
alles des wach und schlafend atmenden Gelds.

O wie mag sie sich schliessen bei Nacht, diese immer
    offene Hand.
Morgen holt sie das Schicksal wieder, und täglich
hält sie es hin: hell, elend, unendlich zerstörbar.

Dass doch einer, ein Schauender, endlich ihren langen Bestand
staunend begriffe und rühmte. Nur dem Aufsingenden säglich.
Nur dem Göttlichen hörbar.

2:19

Somewhere it lives, the gold, in the bank where it's coddled,
and with thousands it seems on intimate terms.
But to even the copper penny, the blind man, the beggar,
is a forgotten, dusty corner under the stairs.

Strolling the rows of shops, gold feels quite at home,
seeming to masquerade there in silks, carnations, and furs.
He, the silent one, stands in the pause between breaths
of all that waking, sleeping, and breathing money.

I imagine it closing at night, that constantly open hand.
Tomorrow fate will summon it back and daily it must
hold out the money: bright, sickly, and infinitely destructible.

Oh, if finally someone—a seer—could, marveling, fathom,
praise, its long existence. Only the singer may say,
and only the god may hear it.

2:20

Zwischen den Sternen, wie weit; und doch, um wievieles
    noch weiter,
was man am Hiesigen lernt.
Einer, zum Beispiel, ein Kind . . . und ein Nächster,
    ein Zweiter –,
o wie unfasslich entfernt.

Schicksal, es misst uns vielleicht mit des Seienden Spanne,
dass es uns fremd erscheint,
denk, wieviel Spannen allein vom Mädchen zum Manne,
wenn es ihn meidet und meint.

Alles ist weit –, und nirgends schliesst sich der Kreis.
Sieh in der Schüssel, auf heiter bereitetem Tische,
seltsam der Fische Gesicht.

Fische sind stumm, meinte man einmal. Wer weiss?
Aber ist nicht am Ende ein Ort, wo man das, was der Fische
Sprache wäre, *ohne* sie spricht?

2:20

Reaching from star to star, what distances! Yet, how much
     farther, still,
what we may learn here and now.
Someone, for instance, a child . . . and next to it, someone else—
could they be farther apart?

Fate perhaps measures us using the span of what is,
so it seems foreign to us.
Think of the spans between woman and man alone,
when she avoids him and loves.

All is far-flung. And the circle closes nowhere.
See on the platter—the table is cheerfully spread—
strange are the fishes' faces.

Fishes are mute, as they used to say. But who knows?
Couldn't there, still, be a place somewhere, where what might
be the fishes' language is spoken *without* them?

2:21

Singe die Gärten, mein Herz, die du nicht kennst; wie in Glas
eingegossene Gärten, klar, unerreichbar.
Wasser und Rosen von Ispahan oder Schiras,
singe sie selig, preise sie, keinem vergleichbar.

Zeige, mein Herz, dass du sie niemals entbehrst.
dass sie dich meinen, ihre reifenden Feigen.
Dass du mit ihren, zwischen den blühenden Zweigen
wie zum Gesicht gesteigerten Lüften verkehrst.

Meide den Irrtum, dass es Entbehrungen gebe,
für den geschehnen Entschluss, diesen: zu sein!
Seidener Faden, kamst du hinein ins Gewebe.

Welchem der Bilder du auch im Innern geeint bist,
(sei es selbst ein Moment aus dem Leben der Pein)
fühl, dass der ganze, der rühmliche Teppich gemeint ist.

2:21

Sing of the gardens, my heart, that you do not know, the gardens
that seem poured into glass—distinct, out of all reach.
Water and roses of Ispahan or of Shiraz,
blissfully sing these incomparable places.

Show, oh, my heart, that you're never in want of them,
and that their figs are ripening just for you,
that through their blossoming boughs you are communing
with their rarefied air, like that of a vision, almost.

Don't ever think that deprivations could follow
on your resolve, once confirmed: the resolve to be!
Now, silken thread, you've come into the weaving.

Whichever innermost image you're joined with,
(even if only a moment out of a long life of pain)
feel that the whole, the praiseworthy carpet's intended.

2:22

O trotz Schicksal: die herrlichen Überflüsse
unseres Daseins, in Parken übergeschäumt, –
oder als steinerne Männer neben die Schlüsse
hoher Portale, unter Balkone gebäumt!

O die eherne Glocke, die ihre Keule
täglich wider den stumpfen Alltag hebt.
Oder die *eine* in Karnak, die Säule, die Säule,
die fast ewige Tempel überlebt.

Heute stürzen die Überschüsse, dieselben,
nur noch als Eile vorbei, aus dem waagrechten gelben
Tag in die blendend mit Licht übertriebene Nacht.

Aber das Rasen zergeht und lässt keine Spuren.
Kurven des Flugs durch die Luft und die, die sie fuhren,
keine vielleicht ist umsonst. Doch nur wie gedacht.

2:22

Oh, despite fate: the magnificent overflowings
of our existence, foaming up out of parks—
or seen as men of stone standing guard at the sides
of high portals, and shouldering balconies.

Oh, and that bell of bronze, with its clapper daily
raised against the dull, the everyday world.
Or that singular one in Karnak, the pillar, the pillar,
almost outlasting even eternal temples.

These days, the overflowings, the same ones exactly
merely rush past us as haste, from horizontal
yellow day into blindingly lit-up night.

But all that racing will pass; it will leave no traces.
Curves of flight through the air and those traveling them,
all, perhaps, have a purpose. That is, if we think they do.

2:23

Rufe mich zu jener deiner Stunden,
die dir unaufhörlich widersteht:
flehend nah wie das Gesicht von Hunden,
aber immer wieder weggedreht,

wenn du meinst, sie endlich zu erfassen.
So Entzogenes ist am meisten dein.
Wir sind frei. Wir wurden dort entlassen,
wo wir meinten, erst begrüsst zu sein.

Bang verlangen wir nach einem Halte,
wir zu Jungen manchmal für das Alte
und zu alt für das, was niemals war.

Wir, gerecht nur, wo wir dennoch preisen,
weil wir, ach, der Ast sind und das Eisen
und das Süsse reifender Gefahr.

2:23

Call on me to help you in the hour
that unceasingly opposes you,
close as faces of imploring dogs,
yet continually turned away

when you think at last you're grasping it.
What's withdrawn like this: most wholly yours.
We are free, for we were turned away
where we thought that we had just been welcomed.

Anxiously we long for footholds,
we, who are too young for what is old,
and too old for things that never were.

We do justice only where we praise.
For we are ourselves the branch and iron;
we, ourselves, are ripening danger's fruit.

2:24

O diese Lust, immer neu, aus gelockertem Lehm!
Niemand beinah hat den frühesten Wagern geholfen.
Städte entstanden trotzdem an beseligten Golfen,
Wasser und Öl füllten die Krüge trotzdem.

Götter, wir planen sie erst in erkühnten Entwürfen,
die uns das mürrische Schicksal wieder zerstört.
Aber sie sind die Unsterblichen. Sehet, wir dürfen
jenen erhorchen, der uns am Ende erhört.

Wir, ein Geschlecht durch Jahrtausende: Mütter und Väter,
immer erfüllter von dem künftigen Kind,
dass es uns einst, übersteigend, erschüttere, später.

Wir, wir unendlich Gewagten, was haben wir Zeit!
Und nur der schweigsame Tod, der weiss, was wir sind
und was er immer gewinnt, wenn er uns leiht.

2:24

Oh, the delight, ever new, in loosened-up loam!
Hardly anyone helped the earliest of the darers.
Cities grew up all the same, lending beauty to shorelines,
jugs filled up with water and oil, all the same.

The gods, we first design them in boldest blueprints,
which are at once destroyed by ill-tempered fate.
But, they are the immortal ones, and at last we will be
hearing the voice of him who will hear us in the end.

We, a race spanning millennia, mothers and fathers,
filled more and more with our developing child,
so it might, some day, surpass and shock us—later.

We, who dare endlessly, oh, how much time we have!
And only taciturn death knows what we are,
and what he always gains by lending us out.

2:25

Schon, horch, hörst du der ersten Harken
Arbeit; wieder den menschlichen Takt
in der verhaltenen Stille der starken
Vorfrühlingserde. Unabgeschmackt

scheint dir das Kommende. Jenes so oft
dir schon Gekommene scheint dir zu kommen
wieder wie Neues. Immer erhofft,
nahmst du es niemals. Es hat dich genommen.

Selbst die Blätter durchwinterter Eichen
scheinen im Abend ein künftiges Braun.
Manchmal geben sich Lüfte ein Zeichen.

Schwarz sind die Sträucher. Doch Haufen von Dünger
lagern als satteres Schwarz in den Aun.
Jede Stunde, die hingeht, wird jünger.

2:25

Come, hear! The first rakes are working already,
sounding that human rhythm again,
in the subdued stillness of strong,
early-spring earth. Coming things seem

fresh and unused. All that so often
already came to you, now seems to come as
if it were new. You always hoped for it,
yet never took it. Instead, it took you.

Even the oak leaves, weathered by winter—
sunset lends future to their dull brown.
Sometimes the breezes signal each other.

Black are the shrubs. But heaps of dung seem
blacker still as they lie on the fields.
Every hour that passes grows younger.

2:26

Wie ergreift uns der Vogelschrei …
Irgendein einmal erschaffenes Schreien.
Aber die Kinder schon, spielend im Freien,
schreien am wirklichen Schreien vorbei.

Schreien den Zufall. In Zwischenräume
dieses, des Weltraums, (in welchen der heile
Vogelschrei eingeht, wie Menschen in Träume)
treiben sie ihre, des Kreischens, Keile.

Wehe, wo sind wir? Immer noch freier,
wie die losgerissenen Drachen
jagen wir halbhoch, mit Rändern von Lachen,

windig zerfetzten. Ordne die Schreier,
singender Gott! dass sie rauschend erwachen,
tragend als Strömung das Haupt und die Leier.

2:26

How it grips us, the cry of the bird . . .
just any once-created cry.
But already the children, playing outside—
they're crying right past the cry that is real.

Their cry is chance. In the in-between spaces
of this, our universe (which, in its wholeness
the bird cry enters, as we enter dreams),
they drive the wedges of their shrieks.

Ah! Where are we? Free—even freer,
high-flying kites that have torn their strings,
we rush halfway up, our edges of laughter

tattered by wind. To these criers bring order,
god of song! Let them waken to be
the current that carries your head and your lyre.

2:27

Giebt es wirklich die Zeit, die zerstörende?
Wann, auf dem ruhenden Berg, zerbricht sie die Burg?
Dieses Herz, das unendlich den Göttern gehörende,
wann vergewaltigts der Demiurg?

Sind wir wirklich so ängstlich Zerbrechliche,
wie uns das Schicksal wahr machen will?
Ist die Kindheit, die tiefe, versprechliche,
in den Wurzeln – später – still?

Ach, das Gespenst des Vergänglichen,
durch die arglos Empfänglichen
geht es, als wär es ein Rauch.

Als die, die wir sind, als die Treibenden
gelten wir doch bei bleibenden
Kräften als göttlicher Brauch.

2:27

Time, that destroyer, could it really exist?
When will it shatter the tranquil mountaintop castle?
And this heart, forever the gods' own possession,
when will it be raped by the demiurge?

Are we really as timid and breakable
as fate is trying to make us believe?
Does childhood, deep, and full of promises,
down in its roots become—later—still?

Ah, the ghost of the transient,
through the naively receptive
it passes as if it were smoke.

As those who we are, the driving ones,
we're still considered by lasting ones
tradition created by gods.

2:28

O komm und geh. Du, fast noch Kind, ergänze
für einen Augenblick die Tanzfigur
zum reinen Sternbild einer jener Tänze
darin wir die dumpf ordnende Natur

vergänglich übertreffen. Denn sie regte
sich völlig hörend nur, da Orpheus sang.
Du warst noch die von damals her Bewegte
und leicht befremdet, wenn ein Baum sich lang

besann, mit dir nach dem Gehör zu gehn.
Du wusstest noch die Stelle, wo die Leier
sich tönend hob –: die unerhörte Mitte.

Für sie versuchtest du die schönen Schritte
und hofftest, einmal zu der heilen Feier
des Freundes Gang und Antlitz hinzudrehn.

2:28

Oh, come and go; you're still a child, almost
yet add a moment's greatness to the dance.
Make it pure constellation of those dances
in which, despite our transience, we surpass

dull orderings of nature; for she stirred
and truly listened only once, when Orpheus sang,
which was when you were set in motion, too,
and puzzled when a tree would long consider

before it came to seek out Hearing with you.
For you still knew the spot at which the lyre
rose and rang out, the unheard, unheard-of center.

The lyre inspired those lovely steps of yours.
You hoped your friend would turn and join his steps
to yours, to share that feast of wholeness.

2:29

Stiller Freund der vielen Fernen, fühle,
wie dein Atem noch den Raum vermehrt.
Im Gebälk der finstern Glockenstühle
lass dich läuten. Das, was an dir zehrt,

wird ein Starkes über dieser Nahrung.
Geh in der Verwandlung aus und ein.
Was ist deine leidendste Erfahrung?
Ist dir Trinken bitter, werde Wein.

Sei in dieser Nacht aus Übermass
Zauberkraft am Kreuzweg deiner Sinne,
ihrer seltsamen Begegnung Sinn.

Und wenn dich das Irdische vergass,
zu der stillen Erde sag: Ich rinne.
Zu dem raschen Wasser sprich: Ich bin.

2:29

Silent friend of far-off places, feel
how your breathing still increases space.
From among the gloomy belfries' beams
let yourself ring out. What feeds on you,

it grows stronger from this sustenance.
Freely enter, freely leave this transformation.
What experience brought you greatest sorrow?
Drinking wine? Then wine you must become.

Be this night devoted to excesses,
magic at the crossroads of your senses;
be the meaning of their strange encounter.

And when earthly things forget you,
to the still earth say, "I'm flowing."
To the rushing water say, "I am."

Rainer Maria Rilke was born in Prague in 1875 and traveled throughout Europe for much of his adult life, returning frequently to Paris. His last years were spent in Switzerland, where he completed his two poetic masterworks, the *Duino Elegies* and the *Sonnets to Orpheus*. He died of leukemia in December 1926.

Christiane Marks came to the U.S. from Germany as a child and holds a BA in Comparative Literature from Earlham College and an MA in German from the University of Cincinnati. A member of the American Translators' Association, Marks has translated historical letters, numerous articles, and two books.

**OPEN
LETTER**

POETRY FROM OPEN LETTER

Per Aage Brandt (Denmark)
If I Were a Suicide Bomber

Eduardo Chirinos (Peru)
The Smoke of Distant Fires

Juan Gelman (Argentina)
Dark Times Filled with Light

Oliverio Girondo (Argentina)
Decals

Lucio Mariani (Italy)
Traces of Time

Henrik Nordbrandt (Denmark)
When We Leave Each Other

Asta Olivia Nordenhof
(Denmark)
The Easiness and the Loneliness

Rainer Maria Rilke (World)
Sonnets to Orpheus

Olga Sedakova (Russia)
In Praise of Poetry

Andrzej Sosnowski (Poland)
Lodgings

Eliot Weinberger (ed.) (World)
Elsewhere

WWW.OPENLETTERBOOKS.ORG